821.914
Sle
Sem

132081

Semmler.
Kenneth Slessor.

**Learning Resources Center
Nazareth College of Rochester, N. Y.**

WRITERS AND THEIR WORK: NO. 194

Kenneth Slessor

by CLEMENT SEMMLER

Published for the British Council
and the National Book League
by Longmans, Green & Co

Two shillings and sixpence net

Kenneth Slessor, born 1901, is by general consent among the foremost of Australian poets and, by the acclaim of some, the best. Australia's most distinguished literary historian, H. M. Green, wrote of his poetic technique that it was 'not only superior to that of any other Australian poet of his generation but comparable at its best with that of any contemporary in England or the United States'.

Mr Semmler who writes in appreciation of Slessor is the Deputy General Manager of the Australian Broadcasting Commission. He is the author of a book of essays and studies, *For the Uncanny Man*, on James Joyce and others; has written monographs on the Australian balladists A. B. 'Banjo' Paterson and Barcroft Boake in the series *Australian Writers and Their Work* and also a full-length biographical study, *The Banjo of the Bush*, the first yet published, on Paterson. As an editor he has made notable contributions to the appreciation of Australian literature, with such collections and anthologies as *Literary Australia*, *A Frank Hardy Swag*, *Stories of the Riverina*, and *Coast to Coast 1965-6* (a biennial collection of Australian short stories). He is at present preparing *Twentieth Century Australian Literary Criticism* for the Oxford University Press. Mr. Semmler is a principal literary reviewer for the *Sydney Morning Herald*, and was for many years associate editor of *Meanjin*, Australia's longest-established literary journal.

Bibliographical Series
of Supplements *to* 'British Book News'
on Writers and Their Work

★

GENERAL EDITOR
Geoffrey Bullough

KENNETH SLESSOR

KENNETH SLESSOR

by

CLEMENT SEMMLER

PUBLISHED FOR
THE BRITISH COUNCIL
AND THE NATIONAL BOOK LEAGUE
BY LONGMANS, GREEN & CO

LONGMANS, GREEN & CO LTD
48 Grosvenor Street, London W.1

*Associated companies, branches and
representatives throughout the world*

First published 1966
First edition © Clement Semmler 1966

*Printed in Great Britain by
F. Mildner & Sons, London, E.C.1*

/32081

CONTENTS

I. INTRODUCTION 7

II. EARLY INFLUENCES 12

III. THE POET OF SYDNEY 23

IV. THE SEA AS IMAGE AND THEME 27

V. THE FINAL PHASE: 1933-44 35

A SELECT BIBLIOGRAPHY 43

Acknowledgments: I am grateful to the following for permission to quote from works in copyright: Messrs Angus and Robertson Ltd. for material from Kenneth Slessor's *Poems*, Dame Mary Gilmore's 'The Shepherd', John Shaw Neilson's 'The Orange Tree', Andrew Barton Paterson's 'A Bushman's Song' and Chris Brennan's 'The Wanderer'; Mr M. B. Yeats and Messrs Macmillan & Co. Ltd. for extracts from 'Sailing to Byzantium' and 'Byzantium' by W. B. Yeats. I should like to say, too, that I found many of the essays and studies on Kenneth Slessor's poetry, listed in the bibliography, helpful and stimulating.

To
NORMAN WILLIAMS

KENNETH SLESSOR

I. INTRODUCTION

Kenneth slessor was born in 1901 in the town of Orange in New South Wales. Nearby was the birthplace of A. B. 'Banjo' Paterson, the most famous of Australian bush balladists thirty-seven years earlier; in this district too some of the richest strikes took place during the gold rushes of the last century. These coincidences of Slessor's birthplace are not unrelated to his place in Australian poetry—and some understanding of the society the poets before him had lived in and the nature of the poetry they produced is necessary to appreciate the more fully his own poetic achievements.

Tiny sections of the coastline of a vast island continent were first settled as penal areas for the 160,000 convicts, mostly of an illiterate peasant and petty-criminal class, transported from the British Isles during the eighty years after the 'First Fleet' arrived in Sydney in 1788. In the harsh environment so created and the harsher one when a few dauntless spirits pushed out into a hostile hinterland there was little scope or reason for cultural pursuits. After the discovery of gold in the eighteen-fifties had attracted to Australia the much needed but polyglot population eventually to become the nucleus of its permanent occupation and economic development, the tasks of hacking out agricultural and pastoral holdings, of forming stable governments, of coping with rapidly growing cities and the social problems thus arising, were again unlikely to nurture the growth of art or literature.

One of the first Australian poets, Charles Harpur, muttered that society about him was only interested in 'money's worth'; there was a ravenous and obsessive hunger for land as realization came of the riches that sheep, cattle and wheat could bring; an acquisitive society in the crudest sense was being established; and there were not even the normal roots being put down to foster an enduring relationship with the soil and consequently a true folk culture. Western technology kept pace with Australian rural development, and machines denied the hard but enduring understanding that many years of patient grappling with the land could bring.

Ironically, a country which began as the dumping ground for the ragtag and bobtail of a highly-integrated aristocratic society rapidly saw its own aristocracy created, an aristocracy of wealth which has formed the basis of Australian society ever since. But the acquisition of wealth in these early days apparently gave no leisure for much else, and J. A. Froude after he had visited Australia in 1886 could write of its people, 'They aim at little except what money will buy, and to make money and buy enjoyment is the be-all and end-all of their existence.'

Yet the voice of poetry was not to be kept down. As a rural industry stabilized itself there had gradually emerged a miscellany of bush-workers (many of them the descendants of emancipated convicts) who as miners, shearers, teamsters, drovers, stockmen and station-hands ('jackaroos') formed an egalitarian society whose abiding bond was 'mateship'. They were, unlike their European counterparts, a nomadic group; but in far-off stations of the outback, around camp-fires, in lonely bush pubs, on the dusty miles of the cattle and sheep-droving tracks, they came together as a ballad community. Their songs, derived from Dublin and London street ballads (through their convict ancestry), from parodies of music-hall songs, and from the crude verses composed among themselves, invariably pointed up their own lives and circumstances. There are many of these bush songs[1] with their characteristic attitudes of admiration for deeds of horsemanship, dislike of the large landholders (the 'squatters') and hero-worship of the bushrangers of the day:

---

[1] For further reference, see especially *Old Bush Songs*, ed. D. Stewart and N. Keesing, and *The Penguin Book of Australian Ballads*, ed. R. Ward.

> He fought six rounds with the horse police until the fatal ball,
> Which pierced his heart with cruel smart, caused Donahoe to
>   fall.
> And as he closed his mournful eyes, he bade this world Adieu
> Saying, 'Convicts all, pray for the soul of Bold Jack Donahoe!'
>   'Bold Jack Donahoe'

Adam Lindsay Gordon (1833-70), an English immigrant at twenty, absorbed sufficient of these bush traditions to write several ballads of outback life; his other mediocre verse is seldom remembered. It is to the dismay of those who hold Australian literature in some regard that because of early misguided enthusiasm his bust stands in Westminster Abbey's Poets' Corner. But Andrew Barton ('Banjo') Paterson (1864-1941) caught from his boyhood an authentic feeling for the Australian bush and especially its people and became the country's most celebrated folk-poet. The first collection of his verses, *The Man from Snowy River* (1895), ran to a number of editions and sold many thousands of copies within a few years—a remarkable achievement within the limited population of the period. Like his contemporaries, the short-lived Barcroft Boake (1866-92) and Henry Lawson (1867-1922) who was better known as a short story writer, he turned out verses which in the most widely-read journal of the day, *The Bulletin*, became the staple poetic diet of most of the literate population of his day and still indeed (as with 'Waltzing Matilda' and 'Clancy of the Overflow') stir the emotions of his countrymen from their schooldays on:

> I'm travellin' down the Castlereagh, and I'm a station-hand;
> I'm handy with the ropin'-pole, I'm handy with the brand,
> And I can ride a rowdy colt, or swing the axe all day,
> But there's no demand for a station-hand along the Castlereagh.
>   So shift, boys, shift, for there isn't the slightest doubt
>   That we've got to make a shift to the stations further out,
>   With the packhorse runnin' after, for he follows like a dog,
>   We must strike across the country at the old jig-jog.
>   'A Bushman's Song'

Such other poetry as had been written was of this narrative kind or at best lyrically descriptive, the latter strongly influenced by Wordsworth, Tennyson and Swinburne. Thus Charles Harpur (1813-68) and Henry Kendall (1839-82). But during the time that the Australian balladists had such a hold, and indeed in the years till the end of the First World War, the readier acceptance of poetry of action, description and narration obscured the work of a talented group of lyric poets whose work has only in more recent years been properly recognized. From their writing lines may be chosen almost at random to illustrate their gifts:

>And he loved the tree
>The sun and the sky,
>And the sound of the wind
>Though he couldn't tell why.
>
>But besides all this
>He loved, to the full,
>The smell of the sheep
>And the greasy wool.
>
>So they buried him out
>(For at last he died)
>Out, all alone
>On a bleak hill-side.
>
>And there's never a sound
>But the bleat of the sheep,
>As they nibble the mound
>That marks his sleep.
>
>Mary Gilmore, 1865-1962: 'The Shepherd'

>The young girl stood beside me. I
>   Saw not what her young eyes could see:
>—A light, she said, not of the sky
>   Lives somewhere in the Orange Tree.

> —Is it, I said, of east or west?
>   The heartbeat of a luminous boy
> Who with his faltering flute confessed
>   Only the edges of his joy?
>
> —Was he, I said, borne to the blue
>   In a mad escapade of Spring
> Ere he could make a fond adieu
>   To his love in the blossoming?
>
> —Listen! the young girl said. There calls
>   No voice, no music beats on me;
> But it is almost sound; it falls
>   This evening on the Orange Tree
>
>   John Shaw Neilson 1872-1942: 'The Orange Tree'

Neilson's talent is astonishing: with no formal education he sang as he was moved in simple but strangely haunting language, ignoring locality, time and fashion.

Standing out, however, as the dominating figure in Australian poetry before Slessor (but an assessment again achieved only by a process of subsequent critical hindsight) was the one who could properly and in his time singularly be called an intellectual and contemplative poet, Christopher Brennan (1870-1932), a university teacher. But Brennan stands apart as well as out from the poets of his era, and from his surroundings, because he scarcely reflected the country he lived in, and was a poet distinctly in the European tradition. Steeped in the inclinations of his own intellectualism, in classical and Biblical mythology, in the Symbolist movement and especially in the work of Mallarmé, his poetic philosophy took shape accordingly. Not only therefore was he a lone peak towering over Australian poetry in general; it was a peak largely inaccessible and seldom climbed. Only lately has a proper consideration of his work been attempted. Since he aligned himself with developments in Western literature that were never fully appreciated in Australia, and since he was, as it were, isolated between two centuries and two hemispheres, his role in Australian poetry seems aptly reflected in his own words:

> I am the wanderer of many years
> who cannot tell if ever he was king
> or if ever kingdoms were: I know I am
> the wanderer of the ways of the worlds,
> to whom the sunshine and the rain are one
> and one to stay or hasten, because he knows
> no ending of the way, no home, no goal,
> and phantom night and grey day alike
> withhold the heart where all my dreams and days
> might faint in soft fire and delicious death.
>
> 'The Wanderer'

These, briefly and imperfectly stated, were the traditions inherited by Slessor when he began writing in the 1920s. The First World War was over and there was an expectation for Australian poetry, prose and drama more favourable than ever before. Education, migration, communications had contrived for a greater literary sophistication; the chief hope of poetry as Judith Wright has observed, 'lay in the sweeping vision Brennan had achieved, the lyricism of Neilson, and the rebellious emphasis on pictorial and sensual qualities in poetry that McCrae had used' along with 'the impetus given by the discovery of the balladic undercurrent in our literature and its popularization in the first years of the century'.[1]

II. EARLY INFLUENCES

There is little in the routine details of Slessor's life relevant to his poetry except that most of it has been spent in Sydney, a city he loves and whose environs as we shall later see enter deeply into his poetry. He was educated at Sydney North Shore Church of England Grammar School and then and up to the present time (except for a short period in Melbourne) has worked with Sydney newspapers. He has

[1] *The Literature of Australia*, ed. Geoffrey Dutton.

edited several poetry anthologies and two literary journals: *Vision* (with Frank Johnson and Jack Lindsay) in 1923 to 1924 and *Southerly* from 1956 to 1961. He was a war correspondent from 1940 to 1943 with Australian troops in Greece, the Near East, Libya and New Guinea, an experience which, except for one magnificent poem, did not appear to have quickened his poetic talent. His name is a corruption of Schloesser, his father's forbears having migrated first from Germany to England. His mother's family was Scottish.

He began writing poetry in his teens; his poems were substantially collected in three early editions: *Earth-Visitors* (1926), *Cuckooz Contrey* (1932) and *Five Bells* (1939). Subsequently a final selection was made by Slessor himself comprising most of these poems, entitled *One Hundred Poems* (1944) re-issued, with the addition of two poems as *Poems* in 1957. On what is therefore at best a slender poetic output and a poetic life which ended in the early 1940s Slessor's reputation rests.

Chronologically, and this is based on Slessor's admission, his output covers three well-defined periods: 1919 to 1926, 1927 to 1932, and from 1932 to the mid-1940s.

A reasonably tidy pattern of poetic development seems to follow. In his youth, as did his older contemporary Hugh McCrae, he fell under the influence of the artist Norman Lindsay who with his brother Jack was a formidable figure in the *avant-garde* of Sydney cultural life in the 1920s. The root of this influence was a determination to cut the bonds of parochialism in popular poetic and artistic affiliations, as demonstrated in the short-lived but important literary magazine *Vision*; to escape the wide open spaces, the horsemanship, the mateship and the limiting horizons of stockdroving, kangaroos and campfires; and to pilot literature and art out into the more exciting waters of cosmopolitanism. One suspects that the driving force in this was unconsciously motivated, a matter of instinct and rebellion rather than positive aim; at any rate, as for Lindsay's paintings, so the material of this poetry was found in the superficial curiosa of romantic reading. The Australian poet-critic A. D. Hope has put it succinctly:

> On a foundation of minor classical mythology—Pan, the satyrs and the centaurs and the nymphs engaged in perpetual games of sexual hide-and-seek, Venus and Cupid, Aristophanes and Petronius—they erected a Middle Ages compounded of Boccaccio, Provençal courts of love, the thieves' kitchens and willing wenches of Villon's Paris and a pantomime version of the Arabian Nights. The Renaissance supplied them with Rabelais and Brantôme's *femmes galantes*, Marlowe's brawling taverns and Shakespeare's Bawdy, the seventeenth century with periwigs and trollops and buccaneers, the eighteenth with Chinoiserie, the spice islands, nabobbery and Macheathery and Hogarthery, and an aristocratic society of the 'sblud and stap-my-vitals school, and ending with the bucks, bruisers and dandies of the Regency and a touch of Baroness Orczy to show that the French revolution had arrived.[1]

Transport this 'curious civilization' to Botany Bay, where Pan and the satyrs disported with nymphs under eucalyptus trees, and 'the Australian Vie de Bohème' was complete. But Slessor in his early verse turned all this into something arrestingly real; I suggest that its impact on the antipodally-removed readers of the 1920s was as unexpected, jarring and yet stimulating as Eliot's early poetry elsewhere. If in retrospect there were signs of a forced whimsy and raffiishness about some of it, there was equally an ecstasy of feeling and wisps of new meaning blowing across existing poetic traditions that suddenly delighted and excited a jaded palate:

> There were strange riders once, came gusting down
> Cloaked in dark furs, with faces grave and sweet,
> And white as air. None knew them, they were strangers—
> Princes gone feasting, barons with gipsy eyes
> And names that rang like viols—perchance, who knows,
> Kings of old Tartary, forgotten, swept from Asia,
> Blown on raven chargers across the world,
> For ever smiling sadly in their beards
>   And stamping abruptly into courtyards at midnight.

[1] 'Slessor 20 Years After', *The Bulletin*, 1 June 1963.

Postboys would run, lanterns hang frostily, horses fume,
The strangers wake the Inn. Men, staring outside
Past watery glass, thick panes, could watch them eat,
Dyed with gold vapours in the candleflame,
Clapping their gloves, and stuck with crusted stones,
Their garments foreign, their talk a strange tongue,
    But sweet as pineapple—it was Archdukes, they must be.

                                      'Earth-Visitors'

    Scaly with poison, bright with flame,
    Great fungi steam beside the gate,
    Run tentacles through flagstone cracks,
    Or claw beyond, where meditate
    Wet poplars on a pitchy lawn.
    Some seignior of colonial fame
    Has planted here a stone-cut faun
        Whose flute juts like a frozen flame.

    O lonely faun, what songs are these
    For skies where no Immortals hide?
    Why finger in this dour abode
    Those Pan-pipes girdled at your side?
    Your Gods, and Hellas too, have passed,
    Forsaken are the Cyclades,
    And surely, faun, you are the last
        To pipe such ancient songs as these.

    Yet, blow you stone-lipped flute, and blow
    Those red-and-silver pipes of Pan.
    Cold stars are bubbling round the moon,
    Which, like some golden Indiaman
    Disgorged by waterspouts and blown
    Through heaven's archipelago,
    Drives orange bows by clouds of stone . . .
        Blow, blow your flute, you stone boy, blow!

                                'Pan at Lane Cove'

    Here was a novel experience piquant to an ordinary appetite; a poetic essence distilled from a romantic mash.

Slessor's superb perception of colours and sounds justified his exoticisms:

> fire fish in the topaz fount
> With red fins blown like water-plants,
> And green cornelian tortoise-rows
> Below the aqueduct, and those
> Gold-feathered cranes, I saw them all.

In Australian poetry had emerged an imagery even more exquisitely formed and unusual than in Shaw Neilson's spontaneous lyricisms: 'kisses like warm guineas of love'; 'that heart which flaps inconstantly,/Like lanthorns in great Winds'; 'maidens like winds of lace,/Tease the dark passages....'; 'the quiet noise of planets feeding'; 'cannons that cry Tirduf, Tirduf....'. Here too was an unheard-of diction: 'wrought-pewter manticores', 'campanili in the town', 'gold ichor', 'painted wyverns'.

In this period Slessor was experimenting with techniques, his 'five-finger exercises' as he has called them. He admitted once that he had especially admired Wilfrid Owen's experiments in rhyming—'easily the most promising of this century'—and spoke of the variations he himself had tried, 'not the matching of consonants only or vowels only but the repetition of a whole syllable both vowels and consonants... The variation of orthodox rhyme ... offers a fascinating study'.

In a sequence called 'Music' his mastery of rhythm and cadence, even in this first period, is astonishingly sure. In the section inspired by Chopin, the remote, unfinished, frustrated feeling of some of his music is suggested by a blending of single and half rhymes (the latter echoing with their vowels but not their consonants) and internal assonance:

> These peaks of stucco, smoking light,
> These Venice-roads, the pools and channels,
> Tunnels the night with a thousand planets
> Daubing their glaze of white ...

> Faintly the dripping, crystal strings
> Unlock their Spanish airs, their festival
> Which, far away, resolves to emptiness,
> Echoes of bitter things.

In the same poem with a verbal energy infectious in itself his verse captures the presto and hurdy-gurdy beat of the scene from Stravinsky's fair; form is used to reflect excitement, movement and colour:

> Up and down the smoke and crying,
> Girls with apple-eyes are flying,
> Country boys in costly braces
> Run with red, pneumatic faces;
> Trumpets gleam, whistles scream,
> Organs cough their coloured steam out.

Equally to be remarked on is his early skill, in these lines from a sonnet, 'Thief of the Moon', to vary and loosen the traditional beat:

> Thief of the moon, thou robber of old delight,
> Thy charms have stolen the star-gold, quenched the moon—
> Cold, cold are the birds that, bubbling out of night,
> Cried once to my ears their unremembered tune—

producing a singing quality which his fellow-poet Ronald McCuaig considers has no parallel in English and is most akin to Verlaine.

Not that some of Slessor's poems in this first period are not gauche in sentiment and trite in expression. He admits this. He would probably prefer to forget lines like:

> Good roaring pistol-boys, brave lads of gold,
> Good roistering easy maids, blown cock-a-hoop
> On floods of tavern-steam, I greet you!

and

> God, whose wings of silver sweep
> Like metal afire on heaven's rim,
> Would daze them with a twinkling peep
> Of those young moon-stained cherubim—

But then most of these poems dealt with a bloodless world; he was writing often sensuously about insensate things, stretching his poetic arms towards the exaggerated elements of experience. 'Young writers,' he said recently in a television interview, 'get their experience secondhand, precariously from what they read. Heine, the Chinese, Sterne, and other writers of his time obsessed me and therefore I was writing about their experiences and not mine. Later . . . you draw from firsthand . . .' The sum of his early verse, much of it brilliant and unusual enough to earn him immediate recognition, was this very journeying from secondhand to firsthand, from romanticism to realism, from in fact a conventional to a highly individual idiom. He was making a style, throwing off the burden of journalism, paying court to the Lindsays, roistering superficially, sorting a subject matter and especially hugging and nurturing his developing talent.

Influences were bound to be apparent in his second period. H. M. Green, the most distinguished of Australian literary historians, states these influences as 'Eliot and the moderns generally' and this is probably so. Slessor as far back as 1931 made no secret of his regard for the poets concerned. 'I would prefer my feelings to be outraged by Mr E. E. Cummings,' he said, 'rather than to have my intellect candied into stupor by Mr Edward Shanks. I regard the silliest, the vulgarest, the crudest of the moderns as of more value than the literary Shintoists who cumber up anthologies with the trancelike worshipping of ancestors'. Perhaps Slessor would take a more mature and balanced view of this now. But he read and admired the poetry of T. S. Eliot (he considered 'The Waste Land' filled with 'the most splendid and haunting rhythms of anything written in our century'), Ezra Pound, Aldington, Sacheverell and Edith Sitwell and especially Wilfred Owen whose experiments in rhythms and rhymes, his carefully arranged schemes of assonance and dissonance in such a poem as 'Strange Meeting', he had closely studied.

It has been argued that the 'romantic grotesquerie' of Slessor's early poems was not simply a passing trait of his earlier days but is a recurring and indeed directing element in his poetry generally. Nobody reading Slessor's poetry as a whole would deny this, but in his later work it is certainly fortified with the infusion of developing everyday experience. Brains were being added to emotion. But in any case Slessor's romanticism was of just that type mentioned by Pater in the Postscript to his 'Appreciations'—the desire of which is 'for a beauty born of unlikely elements'.[1] It is in this respect that much of Slessor's poetry—and especially that of this second period—reminds me of Yeats. Lines from 'Five Visions of Captain Cook':

> Flowers turned to stone! Not all the botany
> Of Joseph Banks, hung pensive in a porthole,
> Could find the Latin for this loveliness,
> Could put the Barrier Reef in a glass box
> Tagged by the horrid Gorgon squint
> Of horticulture. Stone turned to flowers
> It seemed—you'd snap a crystal twig,
> One petal even of the water-garden,
> And have it dying like a cherry-bough.

recall somewhat the extruded romanticism of Yeats in 'Sailing to Byzantium':

> Once out of nature I shall never take
> My bodily form from any natural thing,
> But such a form as Grecian goldsmiths make
> Of hammered gold and gold enamelling
> To keep a drowsy emperor awake,
> Or set upon a golden bough to sing
> To lords and ladies of Byzantium
> Of what is past, or passing, or to come.

Like Yeats, Slessor wrote line after line of quotable verse best described as the 'pure poetry' James Stephens was so

[1] I owe this observation to A. C. W. Mitchell in 'Kenneth Slessor and the Grotesque', *Australian Literary Studies*, December 1964.

fond of talking about; lines in which an unimaginable and inexpressible meaning has been drawn as closely to us as can be contrived, lines of Yeats like

> At midnight on the Emperor's pavement flit
> Flames that no faggot feeds, nor steel has lit,
> Nor storm disturbs, flames begotten of flame

and of Slessor's like

> That street washed with violet
> Writes like a tablet
> Of living here; that pavement
> Is the metal embodiment
> Of living here

Nevertheless, there is an earthier element in much of Slessor's verse of this period, an irony and astringency not so much a matter of literary influences as of the mind taking over from the senses. Much has been made of echoes of T. S. Eliot that crop up in many of these poems. There is the familiar combination of ennui, drouth and wit in his 'Elegy in a Botanic Garden':

> The smell of birds' nests faintly burning
> Is autumn. In the autumn I came
> Where spring had used me better,
> To the clear red pebbles and the men of stone
> And foundered beetles, to the broken Meleager
> And thousands of white circles drifting past,
> Cold suns in water; even to the dead grove
> Where we had kissed, to the Tristamia tree
> Where we had kissed so awkwardly,
> Noted by swans with damp, accusing eyes
> All gone today; only the leaves remain,
> Gaunt paddles ribbed with herring bones
> Of watermelon-pink.

It is almost unintentional parody; more deliberate probably is his curious parody of Eliot's parody of Marvell's 'time's wingèd chariot' couplet:

> Time you must cry farewell, take up the track
> And leave this lovely moment at your back

But these traces are largely coincidental, as are the occasional flashes reminiscent of Pound, Dylan Thomas and others. The simple fact was that he was sharing the disillusion of the poets of his time and expressing it in terms largely individual, but where some overlapping was inevitable. Then again, admiring Eliot's poetry as he has admitted, he undoubtedly found an influence in Eliot's vocabulary and spare style that was at once, as Max Harris has observed in his penetrating monograph on Slessor, wholesome and disciplinary. And, finally, since Slessor had admitted 'no hesitation in using experiment' in 'a breaking of the rules where the fracture can suggest even a shadow of the effect desired', he was naturally quick to respond to the techniques of the early Eliot. Nowhere is the combination of all this better seen than in the first of his four or five major poems, 'Captain Dobbin' (inevitably described by one Australian critic as an 'Eliotan picture of the retired seaman'). The first and last parts of the poem will be sufficient to project its charm and yet sudden vitality, largely the result of its precisely achieved, curiously recondite marine imagery set in its unrhymed and unmetrical sentences and phrases occurring as lines of verse, the 'fracture' of the metre to 'suggest the shadow of the effect desired'. The impact of this on readers of Australian poetry was as dramatic as 'Prufrock' on the wider, transatlantic circle.

> Captain Dobbin, having retired from the South Seas
> In the dumb tides of 1900, with a handful of shells,
> A few poisoned arrows, a cask of pearls,
> And five thousand pounds in the colonial funds,
> Now sails the street in a brick villa, 'Laburnam Villa',
> In whose blank windows the harbour hangs
> Like a fog against the glass,
> Golden and smoky, or stoned with a white glitter,
> And boats go by, suspended in the pane,

> Blue Funnel, Red Funnel, Messageries Maritimes,
> Lugged down the port like sea-beasts taken alive
> That scrape their bellies on sharp sands,
> Of which particulars Captain Dobbin keeps
> A ledger sticky with ink,
> Entries of time and weather, state of the moon,
> Nature of cargo and captain's name,
> For some mysterious and awful purpose
> Never divulged . . . .
>
> Over the flat and painted atlas-leaves
> His reading-glass would tremble,
> Over the fathoms, pricked in tiny rows,
> Water shelving to the coast.
> Quietly the bone-rimmed lens would float
> Till, through the glass, he felt the barbèd rush
> Of bubbles foaming, spied the albicores,
> The blue-finned admirals, heard the wind-swalled cries
> Of planters running on the beach
> Who filched their swags of yams and ambergris,
> Birds' nests and sandalwood.

The elegant final stanza is among the most affecting in Slessor's verse. The old sailor in his last tranquil if pathetic days sits, a shell, among the flotsam and jetsam he has collected. But within the shell are ever the echoes and sounds of the sea, baleful, blind, devouring ships and men on its surface, and the bodies beneath.

> Coldly in the window,
> Like a fog rubbed up and down the glass
> The harbour, bony with mist
> And ropes of water, glittered; and the blind tide
> That crawls it knows not where, nor for what gain,
> Pushed its drowned shoulders against the wheel,
> Against the wheel of the mill.
> Flowers rocked far down
> And white, dead bodies that were anchored there
> In marshes of spent light.
> Blue Funnel, Red Funnel,

> The ships went over them, and bells in engine-rooms
> Cried to their bowels of flaring oil;
> And stokers groaned and sweated with burnt skins,
> Clawed to their shovels.
> But quietly in his room,
> In his little cemetery of sweet essences
> With fond memorial-stones and lines of grace,
> Captain Dobbin went on reading about the sea.

It remains to be said that Captain Dobbin worshipped Cook

> that captain with the sad
> And fine white face, who never lost a man
> Or flinched a peril

and Slessor thus anticipated his other considerable poem of this second phase, 'Five Visions of Captain Cook', which, along with an appreciation of the final period of his verse (from 1933 until the collection of his *One Hundred Poems* in 1944), can be more appropriately left to the last sections of this study.

III. THE POET OF SYDNEY

One might at this point consider Slessor as an 'Australian' poet. As Richard Aldington once noted with some satisfaction, while Slessor wrote genuinely as an Australian he was not a 'professional Aussie'. He was furthest away from the influence, directly or indirectly, of his environment, his landscape, in his earlier verse than in his later; it was as an ironical appreciation of the world about him matured that his verse began to reflect wryly the mores and traditions of his fellow-Australians. At one extreme he could take the laboured, deadly-serious efforts of the early balladists to bush-canonize, with all the trappings of sentimental mateship, Ben Hall, Jack Donahoe, Ned Kelly and their deeds—and with a few swift strokes turn it all into comic strip:

> Jackey Jackey gallops on a horse like a swallow
> Where the carbines bark and the blackboys hollo.
> When the traps give chase (may the Devil take his power!)
> He can ride ten miles in a quarter of an hour.
>
> Take a horse and follow, and you'll hurt no feelings;
> He can fly down waterfalls and jump through ceilings,
> He can shoot off hats, for to have a bit of fun,
> With a bulldog bigger than a buffalo gun....
>
> Flowers in his button-hole and pearls in his pocket,
> He comes like a ghost and he goes like a rocket,
> With a lightfoot heel on a blood-mare's flank
> And a bagful of notes from the Joint Stock Bank.

But at the other end his satire could fix for posterity the country town of the outback (a manifestation more typically Australian than any other) much more truthfully and enduringly than faded photographs yellowing at the edges:

> Country towns, with your willows and squares,
> And farmers bouncing on barrel mares
> To public-houses of yellow wood
> With '1860' over their doors,
> And that mysterious race of Hogans
> Which always keeps General Stores....
>
> Verandahs baked with musky sleep,
> Mulberry faces dozing deep,
> And dogs that lick the sunlight up
> Like paste of gold—or, roused in vain
> By far, mysterious buggy-wheels,
> Lower their ears, and drouse again.

In the middle of these two extremes is the Slessor discreetly Australian—thoughtful rather than intellectual—having discovered his country not so much in spite of as through a period of 'youthful' Bohemianism; having become especially conscious of a region and a place. Subscribing to no national creed he stood off and with the accurate eye of a trained journalist offered, even if only in a few poems, landscapes of unerring detail of the country which had afforded his literary personality its surest coherence—his own Waste Land:

> In the pans of straw-coned country
> This river is the solitary traveller;
> Nothing else moves, the sky lies empty,
> Birds there are none, and cattle not many.
> Now it is sunlight, what is the difference?
> Nothing. The sun is as white as moonlight.
> Wind has buffeted flat the grasses,
> Long, long ago; but now there is nothing.
> Wind gone and men gone, only the water
> Stumbling over the stones in silence.

Here incidentally is a form of verse in which Slessor has tried to express the monotony and loveliness of a stream of water running through vast and lonely plains by using as he has described it 'a flat, monotonous rhythm with a downfall at the end of each line's last double-syllabled word'.

But in such representations there is nothing affectionate; he has kept his love, his poetic enthusiasm and emotion for the city of Sydney. Poets who have found in a particular city the major stimulus of their inspiration are rare in English literature; Slessor remains unique in Australian poetry for this. For many years of his active poetry-writing life he lived in the crowded eastern part of the city built up on higher ground overlooking the Harbour; a skyline of flats and penthouses known as King's Cross. Its main thoroughfare from the city proper is William Street, a minor Broadway of neon signs commemorated by Slessor in a poem of that title, beginning:

> The red globes of light, the liquor-green,
> The pulsing arrows and the running fire
> Spilt on the stones, go deeper than a stream.

Such garish manifestations no less than the city's ugliness —slums, pawnshops, pubs; its noise, smoke and smells ('a blast of onions from the landing')—are cherished in his poetry, even the clanking trams (now a thing of the past) with the strange dimensions of the passing kaleidoscopic world revealed to the poet as passenger:

> And shapes look out, or bodies pass,
> Between the darkness and the flare,
> Between the curtain and the glass,
> Of men and women moving there.
>
> So through the moment's needle-eye,
> Like phantoms in the window-chink,
> Their faces brush you as they fly,
> Fixed in the shutters of a blink.

But most of all there is the Harbour; and Slessor's superbly nostalgic prose evocation[1] helps to explain his poetical preoccupation with it:

The character and the life of Sydney are shaped continually and imperceptibly by the fingers of the Harbour, groping across the piers and jetties, clutching deeply into the hills, the water dyed a whole paint-box's armoury of colour with every breath of air, every shift of light or shade, according to the tide, the clock, the weather and the state of the moon. The water is like silk, like pewter, like blood, like a leopard's skin, and occasionally merely like water. Its pigments run into themselves, from amber and aquamarine through cobalt to the deep and tranquil molasses of a summer midnight. Sometimes it dances with flakes of fire, sometimes it is blank and anonymous with fog, sometimes it shouts as joyously as a mirror. Flights and volleys of yachts drift over it continuously, scattered like the fragments of a white flower, yet forming in the end into the helter-skelter pattern of a race.

Sydney is a kind of dispersed and vaguer Venice . . . at sunset, when the Harbour is glazed with pebbles of gold and white, and the sun is burning out like a bushfire behind Balmain, the ferry-boats put on their lights. They turn into luminous water-beetles, filled with a gliding, sliding reflected glitter that bubbles on the water-like phosphorus . . .

To this haven his roving poetical spirit constantly returns; in the early morning ('bony with mist'), in the hazy noon-day heat, it constantly presents to him its impassiveness, its provocativeness, as in

[1] *A Portrait of Sydney*, ed. G. M. Spencer and S. Ure Smith.

> The sun comes up in a golden stain,
> Floats like a glassy sea-fruit. There is mist everywhere,
> White and humid, and the Harbour is like plated stone.

and

> the quince-bright, bitter slats
> Of sun gone thrusting under Harbour's hair

But most of all at night, and every atom of inspiration Slessor has found in this sweep of water and watercraft, from his high window the focus of his constant observation, is gathered into the nucleus of his art; he carves his phrases in air with an elegance and sensitivity that transmutes Sydney Harbour into every harbour that every poet has loved:

> Darkness comes down. The Harbour shakes its mane,
> Glazed with a leaf of amber; lights appear
> Like thieves too early, dropping their swag by night,
> Red, gold and green, down trap-doors glassy-clear,
> And lanterns over Pinchgut float with light
> Where they so long have lain.
> All this will last, but I who gaze must go
> On water stranger and less clear, and melt
> With flesh away; and stars that I have felt,
> And loved, shall shine for eyes I do not know.

In these lines are woven 'Captain Dobbin' and 'Five Visions of Captain Cook'; his private and personal harbour becomes the all-surrounding Pacific Ocean—the 'water stranger and less clear'; and the flesh to be melted away is of his friend Joe, drowned in the Harbour, whose elegy is Slessor's finest poem, 'Five Bells'.

IV. THE SEA AS IMAGE AND THEME

The sea is more than a theme in Slessor's poetry—it is a dominating image and the subject matter of several of his best-known poems. But he has come to the sea by a number of ways, each of which is in itself a theme recurring frequently in his verse.

The paradoxical relationship of Time and the artist both as an ally and an enemy—as giving a basic theme for art and yet in the end cutting art short—clearly haunted Slessor. It is reflected too in his concern for history and memory, 'the flood that does not flow', and in his musings on eternity. Recently he has deprecated the scientists' habit of juggling with the notion of infinity as but another algebraical symbol: 'Does any mathematician stop to consider what infinity is? The awful thought of infinity?'

> that terrible lane
> Infinity's trapdoor, eternal and merciless.

he has written of it; and yet going back in time to memory gives him no solace either:

> profitless lodgings from the flukes of thought
> Anchored in Time

Occasionally the reference is glossed with irony:

> There's not a moment I can call my own—
> My clocks, my keys, my wheels and instruments
> And that fierce Ethiop, the telephone.

The culmination of this theme is a sequence of three poems, 'Out of Time'. Here the motif coalesces with his larger poetic concept of the sea—and suddenly we are aware that Slessor has found his final symbol for Time that moves destructively and eternally:

> Out of all reckoning, out of dark and light,
> Over the edges of dead Nows and Heres,
> Blindly and softly, as a mistress might,
> He keeps appointments with a million years.
>
> I and the moment laugh, and let him go,
> Leaning against his golden undertow.

> Leaning against the golden undertow,
> Backward, I saw the birds begin to climb
> With bodies hailstone-clear, and shadows flow,
> Fixed in a sweet meniscus, out of Time,
>
> Out of the torrent, like the fainter land
> Lensed in a bubble's ghostly camera,
> The lighted beach, the sharp and china sand,
> Glitters and waters and peninsula—
>
> The moment's world, it was; and I was part,
> Fleshless and ageless, changeless and made free.
> 'Fool, would you leave this country?' cried my heart,
> But I was taken by the suck of sea.
>
> The gulls go down, the body dies and rots,
> And time flows past them like a hundred yachts.

At the close we are reminded of Phlebas the Phoenician, a fortnight dead, who 'forgot the cry of gulls, and the deep sea swell', and that for Eliot too the sea is a strong and central theme. The sea which picked Phlebas' bones in whispers did so too with Joe Lynch lying at the bottom of Sydney Harbour, in 'Five Bells'. Picked bones, the skull, ghosts—these images of death occur especially in Slessor's later verse too, grim tally-men again of the ravages of time, of the mutability of the poet as opposed to the immutability of his work. A small, bare hill is to Slessor as if

> Something below pushed up a knob of skull
> Feeling its way to air

and a cemetery a place where

> tablets cut with dreams of piety
> Rest on the bosoms of a thousand men
> Staked bone by bone, in quiet astonishment
> At cargoes they had never thought to bear

But 'cargoes' again: the sea is never far away.

Why Slessor, a city-based landlubber, should have projected with his poetry his magnificent visions and concepts of the sea, is a question which has brought forward all manner of critical theories. It was, so it has been said, 'his first image of permanence'. With his discovery of the sea 'he became a poet not of frenzy but of calm; not of escapism but of exploration... It drew him because of its separateness from human business... with this natural attraction Slessor's flowing, tidal kind of poetry came gradually to meet and join with its perfect subject.'[1]

I doubt it. It must surely be simpler than that. Slessor lived during what were creatively his most fecund years in an eyrie overlooking Sydney Harbour observing through his window every day and night the scenes and moods of a stretch of water he came to love so passionately. This looking through glass, because it was so regularly part of his daily pattern—'from this perch in the air I could see... the complete history of the sun'—is a recurring and familiar theme in his poetry, even in his earlier verse where he looked for inspiration towards fables and legends. There it is one of the few real, apperceived images as in

> Men, staring outside
> Past watery glass, thick panes

and

> I... spied those ivory courts within
> Through windows of transparent shells.

Gradually the image becomes a deeper, more haunting, more emotional one:

> So the ghost cried, and pressed to the dark pane
> Like a white leaf, his face... in vain... in vain

a world of dead men staring out of glass:

> Look up! Thou hast a shining guest
> Whose body in the dews hath lain,
> His face like a strange wafer pressed
> Secret and starry, at thy pane

[1] Charles Higham in 'The Poetry of Kenneth Slessor', *Quadrant*, Summer 1959-60.

perhaps a symbol of Slessor's own growing sense of disillusionment as he was caught himself by glass barriers between the worlds of reality and the dream.

But the sources of the image can be found in his poetry too—the Harbour below, the watcher above, his days 'tubed in their crystal of soft gaze'. Captain Dobbin, like the poet, watches from his Sydney window 'boats go by suspended in the pane'; the Harbour 'hangs like a fog against the glass'. And in 'Five Bells'—that poem of Slessor's in which all his themes and images meet, the spectre of eternity, the dead man out of the Harbour, comes to the watcher:

> Are you shouting at me, dead man, squeezing your face
> In agonies of speech on speechless panes?
> Cry louder, beat the windows, bawl your name!

Slessor's preoccupation with the sea then is simply the concomitant of his life-long association with the Harbour. He has written of the ships he watched 'all day and most of the night, liners and colliers, tramps and tugs, ships with smears of rust like the red gum of a eucalyptus tree, ships as spick and gleaming as laboratories enter and leave the Heads'. It was thus a natural progression to what lay *beyond* the Heads: the Pacific Ocean and the romantic mysteries of its seas and of Australia's past. As his friend Douglas Stewart, poet, playwright, critic and fellow-associate of the Norman Lindsay salon has put it 'one sees him as a poet at a tower window, sometimes staring down at the water and grinning wryly at his reflection, sometimes gazing out to the blue horizon beyond the Heads and seeing the wraiths of the great voyagers'.[1] Slessor would as lief become the John Benbow of one of his poems

> Walking down William Street
> With a tin trunk and a five pound note, looking for a
>   place to eat,
> And a peajacket the colour of a shark's behind
> That a Jew might buy in the morning

[1] In *The Flesh and the Spirit* (1948).

and to become the poet of the Pacific gave him (as against the confined and by now too familiar environs of the Harbour) a broader canvas to flourish the colours of his imagination:

> dozing houses
> Crammed with black bottles, marish wine
> Crusty and salt-corroded, fading prints,
> Sparkle-daubed almanacs and playing cards,
> With rusty cannon, left by the French outside,
> Half-buried in sand

Inevitably, then, having roved through a somewhat artificial world in his earlier poetry, illimitable in terms of history, the Pacific and Australia now channelled his inspiration into what was poetically a much more viable and reassuring concept, and so he found one of his major subjects, 'The Five Visions of Captain Cook'.

Using a technique more familiar to us through the modern novel and the radio feature Slessor gives us five aspects of Cook, varying his poetic treatment between blank verse (sections I, II and V) and the conventional stanza form (III and IV). Predictably the poem is uneven, a defect compensated for a hundred times by the sweep, power and humanity of his approach. His theme is the classic one of man facing the unknown (and we accept Cook as the archetype of the Australian voyagers, representing no less de Quiros, Torres, Tasman and his other predecessors); his lesson, the futility of it all. As with the bold Tartars and Mongols of his first phase, adventure and high courage end in decay and dust.

Cook, demi-god of navigators, sets off with high purpose and eager ship; the pounding rhythm of the poem's opening represents the pounding of seas against his questing ship:

> Cook was a captain of the powder-days
> When captains, you might have said, if you had been
> Fixed by their glittering stare, half-down the side,
> Or gaping at them up companionways,
> Were more like warlocks than a humble man ...

> Those captains drove their ships
> By their own blood, no laws of schoolbook steam,
> Till yards were sprung and masts went overboard

In the second section Cook's mastery of the oceans is made manifest; the voyage is uneventful. So the rhythm swings easily, confidently and at times disarmingly in a conversational sort of way, denoting that this mission was but after all an exercise in British seamanship:

> Three officers
> In gilt and buttons, languidly on deck
> Pointed their sextants at the sun. One yawned,
> One held a pencil, one put eye to lens;
> Three very peaceful English mariners
> Taking their sights for longitude,
> I've never heard
> Of sailors aching for the longitude
> Of shipwrecks before or since. It was the spell
> Of Cook did this, the phylacteries of Cook.
> Men who ride broomsticks with a mesmerist
> Mock the typhoon. So, too, it was with Cook . . .

Slessor in his early days wrote a good deal of light verse, a medium he mastered with journalistic facility. We have a delightful piece of whimsy about two chronometers. The rhythm is metronomically fitted to the mood, but Slessor hints at the minatory intrusion of the enemy Time:

> Two chronometers the captain had,
> One by Arnold that ran like mad,
> One by Kendal in a walnut case,
> Poor devoted creature with a hangdog face.
>
> Arnold always hurried with a crazed click-click
> Dancing over Greenwich like a lunatic,
> Kendal panted faithfully his watch-dog beat,
> Climbing out of Yesterday with sticky little feet . . .
>
> All through the night-time, clock talked to clock,
> In the captain's cabin, tock-tock-tock,
> One ticked fast and one ticked slow,
> And Time went over them a hundred years ago . . .

The mood of the second part is continued in the fourth, but the free-flowing stanza form hints at the false security of Cook and his men—guns cocked not for the enemy but for game:

> Here, in this jolly-boat they graced,
> Were food and freedom, wind and storm,
> While, fowling-piece across his waist,
> Cook mapped the coast, with one eye cocked for game . . .

Slessor's verse in the final part scales the heights of poetry, as indeed it must to signify the drama and pathos of the end of the adventure, as told here through the senile maunderings and daydreams of Captain Home, one of Cook's officers. Blind and dribbling in his retirement in a Scottish village, Home is a far more pitiful figure than Captain Dobbin:

> This was the port that Alexander Home
> Had come to with his useless cutlass-wounds
> And tales of Cook, and a half-a-crown a day

Even his cronies had heard his tales too often:

> Old Captain-in-the-Corner, drank his rum
> With friendly gestures to four chairs. They stood
> Empty, still warm from haunches, with rubbed nails
> And leather glazed, like aged serving men
> Feeding a king's delight, the sticky, drugged
> Sweet agony of habitual anecdotes.
> But these, his chairs, could bear an old man's tongue,
> Sleep when he slept, be flattering when he woke,
> And wink to hear the same eternal name
> From lips new-dipped in rum.

His wife Elizabeth 'a noble wife but brisk' has heard the story too often, too:

> That's what he lives on, talks on, half-a-crown
> A day, and sits there full of Cook.
> Who'd do your cooking now, I'd like to ask,
> If someone didn't grind her bones away?

But Home has an old man's dreams (his equivalent of Dobbin's marine knick-knacks):

> His body moved
> In Scotland, but his eyes were dazzle-full
> Of skies and water farther round the world—
> Air soaked with blue, so thick it dripped like snow
> On spice-tree boughs, and water diamond-green,
> Beaches wind-glittering with crumbs of gilt,
> And birds more scarlet than a duchy's seal
> That had come whistling long ago and far
> Away

and a terrible memory of the killing which instantly sees the pulse of the verse quicken. Home's recall is razor sharp as he relives the violence and the tragedy:

> the surge of goatish flanks
> Armoured in feathers, like cruel birds:
> Wild, childish faces, killing; a moment seen,
> Marines with crimson coats and puffs of smoke
> Toppling face-down; and a knife of English iron,
> Forged aboard ship, that had been changed for pigs,
> Given back to Cook between the shoulder-blades.

And last the epilogue—recollection in pity and tranquillity and nobility of verse:

> there was nothing left
> Only the sugar-cane and the wild granaries
> Of sand, and palm trees and the flying blood
> Of cardinal-birds; and putting out one hand
> Tremulously in the direction of the beach,
> He felt a chair in Scotland. And sat down.

V. THE FINAL PHASE: 1933-44

With the poetry of his final phase Slessor reached his present reputation as a major Australian poet. It is true that in the years since there have been occasional falls from critical grace, some younger writers regarding this rating as an unproved assumption. On the other hand there are those who consider him the greatest of Australian poets.

Indeed, he has worn well. New readers continue to discover him with enthusiasm; his general readership is maintained; and, certainly in those Australian universities where Australian literature is read, his poetry is usually included in the course of study. Perhaps this is also because his verse presents a tidy front: one collection covers his whole output. It is thus assimilable to the young student who will especially appreciate the poetic elegances, the control of a wide variety of forms (which lend themselves to the sort of analysis currently popular in study-techniques these days) and the agelessness of the poetry; perhaps one can better describe it as a continuing contemporaneity.

Probably some of these considerations prompted H. M. Green's contention that Slessor introduced into Australian poetry 'modernity in both attitude and technique'. This seems an over-simplification. Certainly Brennan before him had introduced much more startling techniques of symbolism and surrealism. But the years of the First World War distracted attention from Brennan's work; Slessor on the other hand burst like a meteor on a post-war society eager for a life and literature hitherto disrupted. And at this important watershed it was not a continuing stream of the ballad nor of the uncomplicated lyricism of Mary Gilmore and others that was looked for. The jazz age and postwar restlessness which affected Australia no less than the rest of the world demanded even in its poetry something more startling.

Slessor answered this with a 'poetic expressionism'; an art which annihilated natural expectations and environment and offered new experiments to some extent in form but most of all in imagery. Herein lay his modernism since, as Max Harris has aptly put it, 'he had a native talent for the effective and often startling image and the modern movement allowed him those touches of verbal bravura which he so obviously enjoyed'. Slessor's expressionism leaned heavily on the telescoping of images, the sudden fusion of their unusual elements: 'the naphtha flash of lightning slit the sky/Knifing the dark with deathly photographs'; 'the great Miser, Night,/Rubbing a mountain's breast-bone/With an old rind of light'; 'the soft strings/Of Death with leather jaws come tasting men'. There is his constant emphasis—magnified in his longer poems—upon emotion as opposed to intellectuality; and in his later poems especially an exploitation of disillusionment and despair as opposed to faith. Above all there is a continuing irony, a quality which above most others has distinguished modern Australian poetry:

> Who could have called that soft, adhesive nag
> We bounced our lives on, a wild horse?

But added to this Slessor worked hard at his poetry (probably harder than any Australian poet before him) always experimenting, always obsessed with poetry as a craft. Perhaps his continual association with the printed word had something to do with this. But in his few statements on his poetry he has always come back to this point of grappling with his medium:

> I do know what I have wanted to do and I know as well, often bitterly, how far I have failed to do it . . . Sometimes I please myself by experiment, sometimes I revolt and flagellate myself. But I must write for myself, and speak for myself, and that is why writing poetry is still, I think, a pleasure out of hell.

It is this combination, imagery, experiment, technique, with an unusual capacity for self-criticism (a quality which is quite simply the answer to the so-called riddle of his abrupt decision twenty years ago not to go on writing poetry) which makes for Slessor's individuality as a poet. Of all the Australian poets who have written during this century he can least be confused with any other. No better illustration of this can be offered than one of his later poems, 'Sleep', a technical masterpiece compellingly Slessorian. He combines the themes of birth, life, love and death, through the device of Sleep addressing sleeper, woman her lover, and mother her unborn baby, maintaining magnificently throughout the paramount image of the sleep-womb relationship, with mood and sound corresponding. The thudding insistence of the third stanza's climax with the internal half-rhymes of 'clamber', 'slumber', 'dumb chamber' and the onomatopoeia that follows, conveys unforgettably Slessor's central idea of the prisoner, whether foetus, sleeper, or human being, beating against the walls of his dungeon:

> Do you give yourself to me utterly,
>   Body and no-body, flesh and no-flesh,
> Not as a fugitive, blindly or bitterly,
>   But as a child might, with no other wish?
> Yes, *utterly*.
>
> Then I shall bear you down my estuary,
> Carry you and ferry you to burial mysteriously,
> Take you and receive you,
> Consume you, engulf you,
> In the huge cave, my belly, lave you
> With huger waves continually.
>
> And you shall cling, and clamber there
> And slumber there, in that dumb chamber,
> Beat with my blood's beat, hear my heart move
> Blindly in bones that ride above you,
> Delve in my flesh, dissolved and bedded,
> Through viewless valves embodied so—
>
> Till daylight, the expulsion and awakening,
>   The riving and the driving forth,
> Life with remorseless forceps beckoning—
>   Pangs and betrayal of harsh birth.

But the poem by which Slessor is best known to his Australian audience, 'Five Bells', reflects more truly his mental and emotional complex and his poetic personality, and in its imagery is a final fusing of all the themes referred to earlier in this essay. 'Five Bells' is the coping-stone of his verse. Even his keenest critics have conceded it to be one of the two or three best poems written in Australia.

It is an elegy of a particular kind. It has been compared to Arnold's 'Thyrsis' and 'The Scholar Gipsy', and at least there is nothing absurd about this since it is a recognition that Slessor's poem is impressive enough to be judged in the best company. It is an elegy foreshadowed in lines Slessor had written many years before:

> There are still fields to meet the morning on,
> But those who made them beautiful have gone.

It is as much an elegy on his personal poetry, on his earlier life in Sydney and the years of his verse-making as it is on his dead friend and newspaper colleague Joe Lynch, drowned in Sydney Harbour.

> *Time that is moved by little fidget wheels*
> *Is not my Time, the flood that does not flow.*
> *Between the double and the single bell*
> *Of a ship's hour, between a round of bells*
> *From the dark warship riding there below,*
> *I have lived many lives, and this one life*
> *Of Joe, long dead, who lives between five bells.*
>
> Deep and dissolving verticals of light
> Ferry the falls of moonshine down. Five bells
> Coldly rung out in a machine's voice. Night and water
> Pour to one rip of darkness, the Harbour floats
> In air, the Cross hangs upside-down in water.
>
> Why do I think of you, dead man, why thieve
> These profitless lodgings from the flukes of thought
> Anchored in Time? You have gone from earth,
> Gone even from the meaning of a name;
> Yet something's there, yet something forms its lips
> And hits and cries against the ports of space,
> Beating their sides to make its fury heard.

Here in the form of a dramatic, meditative monologue, with undulating rhythms and repetitions achieving a splendid, solemn music, is a poetic capsule in which is concentrated the essence of everything Slessor has had to say, and his manner of saying it. The Harbour, clutching hand of the Pacific, has with its 'black thumb-balls' crushed the life of Joe Lynch; Time has won again; five bells toll for one man whose death diminishes Slessor as well as mankind, but Slessor is thinking of his own death especially—death which will reduce him to 'some bones/long shoved away';

> But I hear nothing, nothing ... only bells.
> Five bells, the bumpkin calculus of Time.
> Your echoes die, your voice is dowsed by Life,
> There's not a mouth can fly the pygmy strait—
> Nothing except the memory of some bones
> Long shoved away, and sucked away, in mud;
> And unimportant things you might have done.
> Or once I thought you did.

Slessor mourns that (using the inevitable progress of his earlier imagery on this theme) he cannot 'break the glass' and relive their friendship, their arguments on 'Milton, melons and the Rights of Man', a bush walk at night, a stay in Melbourne, their life shared in Sydney:

> by the spent aquarium-flare
> of penny gaslight on pink wallpaper.

Once again Slessor turns his face to the Harbour:

> Where have you gone? The tide is over you.
> The turn of midnight water's over you,
> As Time is over you, and mystery,
> And memory, the flood that does not flow.
> You have no suburb, like those easier dead
> In private berths of dissolution laid—
> The tide goes over, the waves ride over you
> And let their shadows down like shining hair.
> But they are Water; and the sea-pinks bend
> Like lilies in your teeth, but they are weed;
> And you are only part of an Idea.
> I felt the wet push its black thumb-balls in,
> The night you died, I felt your eardrums crack,
> And the short agony, the longer dream,

> The Nothing that was neither long nor short;
> But I was bound, and could not go that way,
> But I was blind, and could not feel your hand.
> If I could find an answer, could only find
> Your meaning, or could say why you were here
> Who now are gone, what purpose gave you breath
> Or seized it back, might I not hear your voice?

Here is complete empathy surrounded by a poetical mood not of self-pity but of anguish, not so much of melancholy as of utter weariness. The moment is over; the water laps Joe's body. Slessor looks for the last time out of his windows and concludes his elegy not with the Chian wine, the green bursting figs, and the blue Midland waters of 'The Scholar Gipsy' nor with a vision of the 'loved hill-side' where Arnold sought peace with Clough, but with a music no less profound. The wheel of life and the spiral of Time has brought him back in final contemplation of the Harbour and its night-sounds:

> I looked out of my window in the dark
> At waves with diamond quills and combs of light
> That arched their mackerel-backs and smacked the sand
> In the moon's drench, that straight enormous glaze,
> And ships far off asleep, and Harbour buoys
> Tossing their fireballs wearily each to each,
> And tried to hear your voice, but all I heard
> Was a boat's whistle, and the scraping squeal
> Of seabird's voices far away, and bells,
> Five bells. Five bells coldly ringing out.
>
> 'Five Bells'

This is Slessor's fitting and farewell statement of his poetry. But there is a postscript. His few years abroad with the Australian forces prompted him out of pity for a useless slaughter to find a final occasion for poetry, to write an elegy for an unknown sailor. It is the simplest possible poetic statement: that soldiers die and are buried; but it is also an epitaph on his own body of verse inscribed with every felicity of structure and language he is capable of. This poem, 'Beach Burial' (conceived near El Alamein in 1942) seems to me the apotheosis of his best poetic achievement: he has written words which mean something greater than their meaning, which give a sudden glimpse of the whole of experience, and in so doing make us, the readers, part of this momentary exaltation:

> Softly and humbly to the Gulf of Arabs
> The convoys of dead sailors come;
> At night they sway and wander in the waters far under,
> But morning rolls them in the foam.
>
> Between the sob and clubbing of the gunfire
> Someone, it seems, has time for this,
> To pluck them from the shallows and bury them in burrows
> And tread the sand upon their nakedness;
>
> And each cross, the driven stake of tidewood,
> Bears the last signature of men,
> Written with such perplexity, with such bewildered pity,
> The words choke as they begin—
>
> *Unknown seaman*—the ghostly pencil
> Wavers and fades, the purple drips,
> The breath of the wet season has washed their inscriptions
> As blue as drowned men's lips.
>
> Dead seamen, gone in search of the same landfall,
> Whether as enemies they fought,
> Or fought with us, or neither; the sand joins them together,
> Enlisted on the other front.

KENNETH SLESSOR
A Select Bibliography
(Place of publication Sydney)

Bibliography
A GUIDE TO TEN AUSTRALIAN POETS, by H. Anderson (1953)
—includes a bibliography of Slessor's works to 1952.

Collected Works:
ONE HUNDRED POEMS (1944).
POEMS (1957)
—a re-issue of *One Hundred Poems* with two additional poems.

Separate Works:
POETRY IN AUSTRALIA, ed. (1923). *Anthology*
THIEF OF THE MOON (1924). *Verse*
EARTH VISITORS. London (1926). *Verse*
FUNNY FARMYARD (1931). *Light Verse*
CUCKOOZ CONTREY (1932). *Verse*
DARLINGHURST NIGHTS (1933). *Light Verse*
FIVE BELLS (1939). *Verse*
POETRY IN AUSTRALIA, ed. (1945). *Anthology*
THE PENGUIN BOOK OF AUSTRALIAN VERSE, ed. with R. G. Howarth and J. Thompson (1958). *Anthology*

Articles:
'Modern English Poetry'. *Australian-English Association Offprint*, 9. October, 1931
—text of address to the Association.
'Writing Poetry: The How and the Why'. *Southerly*, 3, 1948
—text of an Australian Broadcasting Commission broadcast.
A PORTRAIT OF SYDNEY, ed. G. M. Spencer and S. Ure Smith (1950)
—contains essay 'A Portrait of Sydney'.
'Australian Poetry and Hugh McCrae'. *Southerly*, 3, 1956.
Note: K. Slessor edited *Vision*, with F. Johnson and J. Lindsay, from 1923 to 1924, and *Southerly* from 1956 to 1961.

Some Biographical and Critical Studies:
KENNETH SLESSOR, by M. Harris (1963)
—a monograph. The only sustained study to date of Slessor's verse.

TALES OUT OF BED, by R. McCuaig (1944)
—includes a study of Kenneth Slessor originally printed in *The Bulletin*, 9 August 1939. This is one of the first and best appreciations of Slessor's verse.

FOURTEEN MINUTES, by H. M. Green (1944)
—includes a study of Kenneth Slessor.

'Kenneth Slessor', by T. Inglish Moore. *Southerly*, 4, 1947.

THE FLESH AND THE SPIRIT, by D. Stewart (1948)
—includes 'Harbour and Ocean', a most perceptive appreciation of Slessor's poetry.

'Poetry in Australasia—Kenneth Slessor', by P. Lindsay. *The Poetry Review*, 40. London, 1949.

'Sound in Slessor's Poetry', by R. G. Howarth. *Southerly*, 4, 1955
—a fine analysis of Slessor's diction and technique.

ESSAYS IN POETRY, by V. Buckley. Melbourne (1957)
—includes 'Kenneth Slessor: Realist or Romantic?', a valuable study of Slessor in the context of modern Australian verse.

'The Poetry of Kenneth Slessor', by F. T. Macartney. *Meanjin*, Spring, 1957.

'Kenneth Slessor', by R. Aldington. *Australian Letters*, April, 1958.

'The Poetry of Kenneth Slessor', by C. Higham. *Quadrant*, Summer, 1959-60
—a stimulating and provocative essay.

'Slessor Twenty Years After', by A. D. Hope. *The Bulletin*, 1 June 1960.

A HISTORY OF AUSTRALIAN LITERATURE, by H. M. Green (1961)
—Vol. I, pp. 855-89, a most useful outline of Slessor's verse.

'Kenneth Slessor: Television Interview with J. Thompson'. Transcript, Australian Broadcasting Commission (1964).

THE LITERATURE OF AUSTRALIA, ed. G. Dutton (1964)
—includes 'Kenneth Slessor and the Powers of Language' by C. Wallace-Crabbe.

'Kenneth Slessor and the Grotesque', by A. C. W. Mitchell. *Australian Literary Studies*, December 1964.

WRITERS AND THEIR WORK
General Editor: GEOFFREY BULLOUGH

The first 55 issues in the Series appeared under the General Editorship of T. O. BEACHCROFT
Issues 56-169 appeared under the General Editorship of BONAMY DOBRÉE

General Surveys:
THE DETECTIVE STORY IN BRITAIN: Julian Symons
THE ENGLISH BIBLE: Donald Coggan
ENGLISH VERSE EPIGRAM: G. Rostrevor Hamilton
ENGLISH HYMNS: A. Pollard
ENGLISH MARITIME WRITING: Hakluyt to Cook: Oliver Warner
THE ENGLISH SHORT STORY I: & II: T. O. Beachcroft
THE ENGLISH SONNET: Patrick Cruttwell
ENGLISH SERMONS: Arthur Pollard
ENGLISH TRAVELLERS IN THE NEAR EAST: Robin Fedden
THREE WOMEN DIARISTS: M. Willy

Sixteenth Century and Earlier:
FRANCIS BACON: J. Max Patrick
CHAUCER: Nevill Coghill
THOMAS KYD: Philip Edwards
LANGLAND: Nevill Coghill
MALORY: M. C. Bradbrook
MARLOWE: Philip Henderson
MORE: E. E. Reynolds
RALEGH: Agnes Latham
SIDNEY: Kenneth Muir
SKELTON: Peter Green
SPENSER: Rosemary Freeman
WYATT: Sergio Baldi

Seventeenth Century:
SIR THOMAS BROWNE: Peter Green
BUNYAN: Henri Talon
CAVALIER POETS: Robin Skelton
CONGREVE: Bonamy Dobrée
DONNE: F. Kermode
DRYDEN: Bonamy Dobrée
ENGLISH DIARISTS: Evelyn and Pepys: M. Willy
FARQUHAR: A. J. Farmer
JOHN FORD: Clifford Leech
GEORGE HERBERT: T. S. Eliot
HERRICK: John Press
HOBBES: T. E. Jessop
BEN JONSON: J. B. Bamborough
LOCKE: Maurice Cranston
ANDREW MARVELL: John Press
MILTON: E. M. W. Tillyard
RESTORATION COURT POETS: V. de S. Pinto
SHAKESPEARE: C. J. Sisson
SHAKESPEARE: CHRONICLES: Clifford Leech
EARLY COMEDIES: Derek Traversi
FINAL PLAYS: F. Kermode
GREAT TRAGEDIES: Kenneth Muir
HISTORIES: L. C. Knights
LATER COMEDIES: G. K. Hunter
POEMS: F. T. Prince
PROBLEM PLAYS: Peter Ure
ROMAN PLAYS: T. J. B. Spencer
THREE METAPHYSICAL POETS: Margaret Willy
IZAAK WALTON: Margaret Bottrall
WEBSTER: Ian Scott-Kilvert
WYCHERLEY: P. F. Vernon

Eighteenth Century:
BERKELEY: T. E. Jessop
BLAKE: Kathleen Raine
BOSWELL: P. A. W. Collins
BURKE: T. E. Utley
BURNS: David Daiches
WM. COLLINS: Oswald Doughty
COWPER: N. Nicholson
CRABBE: R. L. Brett
DEFOE: J. R. Sutherland
FIELDING: John Butt
GAY: Oliver Warner
GIBBON: C. V. Wedgwood
GOLDSMITH: A. Norman Jeffares
GRAY: R. W. Ketton-Cremer
HUME: Montgomery Belgion
JOHNSON: S. C. Roberts
POPE: Ian Jack
RICHARDSON: R. F. Brissenden
SHERIDAN: W. A. Darlington
CHRISTOPHER SMART: G. Grigson
SMOLLETT: Laurence Brander
STEELE AND ADDISON: A. R. Humphreys
STERNE: D. W. Jefferson
SWIFT: J. Middleton Murry
HORACE WALPOLE: Hugh Honour

Nineteenth Century:
MATTHEW ARNOLD: Kenneth Allott
JANE AUSTEN: S. Townsend Warner
BAGEHOT: N. St. John-Stevas
THE BRONTË SISTERS: P. Bentley
BROWNING: John Bryson
ELIZABETH BARRETT BROWNING: Alethea Hayter
SAMUEL BUTLER: G. D. H. Cole
BYRON: Herbert Read
CARLYLE: David Gascoyne
LEWIS CARROLL: Derek Hudson
CLOUGH: Isobel Armstrong

COLERIDGE: Kathleen Raine
DE QUINCEY: Hugh Sykes Davies
DICKENS: K. J. Fielding
DISRAELI: Paul Bloomfield
GEORGE ELIOT: Lettice Cooper
SUSAN FERRIER & JOHN GALT:
    W. M. Parker
FITZGERALD: Joanna Richardson
MRS. GASKELL: Miriam Allott
GISSING: A. C. Ward
THOMAS HARDY: R. A. Scott-James
    and C. Day Lewis
HAZLITT: J. B. Priestley
HOOD: Laurence Brander
G. M. HOPKINS: Geoffrey Grigson
T. H. HUXLEY: William Irvine
KEATS: Edmund Blunden
LAMB: Edmund Blunden
LANDOR: G. Rostrevor Hamilton
EDWARD LEAR: Joanna Richardson
MACAULAY: G. R. Potter
MEREDITH: Phyllis Bartlett
JOHN STUART MILL: M. Cranston
WILLIAM MORRIS: P. Henderson
NEWMAN: J. M. Cameron
PATER: Iain Fletcher
PEACOCK: J. I. M. Stewart
ROSSETTI: Oswald Doughty
CHRISTINA ROSSETTI:
    Georgina Battiscombe
RUSKIN: Peter Quennell
SIR WALTER SCOTT: Ian Jack
SHELLEY: Stephen Spender
SOUTHEY: Geoffrey Carnall
R. L. STEVENSON: G. B. Stern
SWINBURNE: H. J. C. Grierson
TENNYSON: F. L. Lucas
THACKERAY: Laurence Brander
FRANCIS THOMPSON: P. Butter
TROLLOPE: Hugh Sykes Davies
OSCAR WILDE: James Laver
WORDSWORTH: Helen Darbishire
Twentieth Century:
W. H. AUDEN: Richard Hoggart
HILAIRE BELLOC: Renée Haynes
ARNOLD BENNETT: F. Swinnerton
EDMUND BLUNDEN: Alec M. Hardie
ELIZABETH BOWEN: Jocelyn Brooke
ROBERT BRIDGES: J. Sparrow
ROY CAMPBELL: David Wright
JOYCE CARY: Walter Allen
G. K. CHESTERTON: C. Hollis
WINSTON CHURCHILL: John Connell
R. G. COLLINGWOOD: E.W.F. Tomlin
I. COMPTON-BURNETT:
    Pamela Hansford Johnson

JOSEPH CONRAD: Oliver Warner
WALTER DE LA MARE: K. Hopkins
NORMAN DOUGLAS: Ian Greenlees
T. S. ELIOT: M. C. Bradbrook
FIRBANK & BETJEMAN: J. Brooke
FORD MADOX FORD: Kenneth Young
E. M. FORSTER: Rex Warner
CHRISTOPHER FRY: Derek Stanford
JOHN GALSWORTHY: R. H. Mottram
ROBERT GRAVES: M. Seymour-Smith
GRAHAM GREENE: Francis Wyndham
L. P. HARTLEY & ANTHONY POWELL:
    P. Bloomfield and B. Bergonzi
A. E. HOUSMAN: Ian Scott-Kilvert
ALDOUS HUXLEY: Jocelyn Brooke
HENRY JAMES: Michael Swan
JAMES JOYCE: J. I. M. Stewart
RUDYARD KIPLING: Bonamy Dobrée
D. H. LAWRENCE: Kenneth Young
C. DAY LEWIS: Clifford Dyment
WYNDHAM LEWIS: E. W. F. Tomlin
LOUIS MACNEICE: John Press
KATHERINE MANSFIELD: Ian Gordon
JOHN MASEFIELD: L. A. G. Strong
SOMERSET MAUGHAM: J. Brophy
GEORGE MOORE: A. Norman Jeffares
EDWIN MUIR: J. C. Hall
J. MIDDLETON MURRY: Philip Mairet
GEORGE ORWELL: Tom Hopkinson
POETS OF 1939-45 WAR:
    R. N. Currey
POWYS BROTHERS: R. C. Churchill
J. B. PRIESTLEY: Ivor Brown
HERBERT READ: Francis Berry
FOUR REALIST NOVELISTS:
    Vincent Brome
BERTRAND RUSSELL: Alan Dorward
BERNARD SHAW: A. C. Ward
EDITH SITWELL: John Lehmann
OSBERT SITWELL: Roger Fulford
C. P. SNOW: William Cooper
STRACHEY: R. A. Scott-James
SYNGE & LADY GREGORY:
    Elizabeth Coxhead
DYLAN THOMAS: G. S. Fraser
EDWARD THOMAS: Vernon Scannell
G. M. TREVELYAN: J. H. Plumb
WAR POETS: 1914-18: E. Blunden
EVELYN WAUGH: Christopher Hollis
H. G. WELLS: Montgomery Belgion
PATRICK WHITE: R. F. Brissenden
CHARLES WILLIAMS: J. Heath-Stubbs
VIRGINIA WOOLF: B. Blackstone
W. B. YEATS: G. S. Fraser
ANDREW YOUNG & R. S. THOMAS:
    L. Clark and R. G. Thomas